The Society for the Humanities
Cornell University

Studies in the Humanities I

THE MORALITY OF SCHOLARSHIP

The Morality
of Scholarship

by NORTHROP FRYE
STUART HAMPSHIRE
CONOR CRUISE O'BRIEN

EDITED BY
Max Black

Cornell University Press
Ithaca, New York

Foreword

The following papers were read at the formal inauguration, on October 27, 1966, of The Society for the Humanities. The topic was suggested by Lionel Trilling's essay "The Two Environments," which appeared in *Encounter* in July 1965 and has since been reprinted in Trilling's book *Beyond Culture* (New York: Viking, 1965). In that essay, Mr. Trilling wondered whether the study of literature could still be justified, in the spirit of Sidgwick and Arnold, as having a "unique effectiveness in opening the mind and illuminating it, in purging the mind of prejudices and received ideas, in making the mind free and active." The task of chastening the philistine has been too successfully accomplished: young minds have been so purged of "prejudices and received ideas" (for most of them a distinction without a difference) and so alienated from the "values" expressed in the threadbare rhetoric of political exhortation, that it would be a work of supererogation to rid them of any illusions, except that of being free from illusions. Modern literature, history, and analytic philosophy seem only to confirm the congenial relativism and nihilism that students bring to the study of these "humanities." Too often abetted by teachers who are equally perplexed, they readily turn to safe questions of style, or to anything else that falls within the scope of "objective scholarship." The sacred autonomy of art and science becomes a pretext for converting what still claims, in the old style, to be "an improvement of the intelligence, and especially the intelligence as it touches the moral life" into an entertaining game, dissociated from the problems of conduct, the ordering of the good life, and the individual's relations to society.

What becomes then of the traditional "liberalizing and humanizing" goal of the humanities? Can the contemporary writer and the contemporary scholar be satisfied to adopt a posture of "systematic irreverence, . . . the desire, the insistence, to test for relevance, above all for truth, any idea . . . and if it is found wanting, to reject it without more ado"? [1] Does the whole duty of the "humanist" imply more than this? If so, how is that duty to be defined? Can a humanist "take sides," even on behalf of systematic irreverence, without appeal to ulterior and perhaps aesthetically and educationally irrelevant standards? Is there a risk of a new *trahison des clercs?*

It was to such questions as these that the symposiasts

[1] Richard Wollheim, *On Drawing an Object* (London, 1964).

were invited to address themselves. Given the dedication of The Society for the Humanities to the encouragement of fundamental debate concerning the nature, scope, function, and educational implications of the humanities, it seemed a reasonably promising way of provoking some good discussion about important issues.

All three papers, and especially the first two, illustrate the fragile complexity of such questions about scholarly commitments. Only an exceptionally self-satisfied scholar could stand pat, nowadays, on the traditional virtues of detachment, fidelity to the truth, and a lofty indifference to consequences. Treated as unanalyzable surds, these admirable ideals threaten to degenerate into the cant phrases of still another rhetoric, no less shabby for the unction of its delivery. It is all very well for another speaker on the same occasion to declare: "I don't really believe in the morality of scholarship at all. I believe much more profoundly in the immorality of scholarship. I think it has a brutal but simple obligation to slash through the swathings of moral cocoonery in which mankind is constantly draping the ugly, ordinary, necessary facts of its ignobly decent or indecent existence. I believe scholarship has an obligation to the real, and to nothing else." [2] If evidence were needed that this is itself a moral protest, for all its half-serious protestation of neutrality, the vocabulary of "obligation," "brutal," "ignobly," and

[2] Robert M. Adams.

"decent" would make the point. But is this kind of moral position uniquely self-validating, needing neither defense nor explication?

The "real"—or the "*really* real," as students like to say—bears no engraved credentials of authenticity. Mr. O'Brien's valuable paper astringently points out the degree to which uncritical adherence to an ideal of objectivity may lead scholars to aid inhuman policies, which they would be eager to disavow in their political moments. His indictment is all the more telling if we grant the targets of his criticism the balm of good faith and an undisturbed conscience. Some of O'Brien's readers may resent his charge of "counterrevolutionary subordination" or his description of "a society maimed through the systematic corruption of its intelligence, to the accompaniment of piped music." But his accusations are too specific and too well documented to be merely shrugged aside. An important part of the morality of scholarship may demand a willingness to consider, more seriously than is customary, the social and political implications of designs for research. Scholars unwilling to accept O'Brien's description of their morality as "that of the advanced, capitalistic world" might well consider themselves obligated to elaborate and justify some alternative conception.

Trilling, in the article to which I have already referred, observes that "if literature (or art in general) has indeed become a religion, at least in a manner of speaking, it is true that those who profess it make scarcely any demand upon it for those rational and consequential elements that have been thought essential to highly developed religions." The reproach would remain pertinent with the substitution of "the humanities" for "literature" and "morality" for "religion." Trilling adds that the "ethic" of the "literary religion," though difficult to present systematically, "is by no means obscure." That he is overoptimistic in this estimate, the suggestive papers of Mr. Frye and Mr. Hampshire strongly indicate.

A great merit of these distinguished essays is their implicit recognition of the need to construct some general conceptual framework (Frye would call it—nonpejoratively, I think—a "myth") within which the questions here raised can be profitably discussed. The commentator whom I have already quoted as rejecting a morality of scholarship also said that "all scholars of the humanist persuasion are explicitly or implicitly metaphysicians." But the only respectable metaphysics, in the somewhat popular sense in question, is an explicit one.

Intimations of such a metaphysics (or "myth," or "model") are present in Frye's impressive essay. He may not have altogether avoided that "naïve ferocity of abstractions" which he warns against, in his comparison of artistic "craftmanship" with scientific "objectivity," and in his sharp contrast between "detachment" and "concern" (defined, in broad strokes, as "the preference of life, freedom, and happiness to their opposites"). His imputation of scientific involvement with the merely "phenomenological" might strike some readers as oversimplified. But those familiar with the body of Frye's subtle and closely argued writings will hardly need telling how much solid doctrine stands behind his *obiter dicta*.

Whereas Frye stresses the side of morality which demands a "sense of the kind of obligation that enables man to preserve his relation to society," Mr. Hampshire reminds us of morality's relevance to "the individual's own defense against, and control of, his original, and now often unfitting, instincts, and of the primary emotions and impulses derived from them." Both writers recognize a permanent, and perhaps ultimately unresolvable, tension between the moral demands of "concern"—whether for others or for what Hampshire calls the "inner life of hoarded feeling"— and the necessary "displacement" or "indirection" of imaginative scholarship. Hampshire's observation that "concern is always concern for an object recognized as *independent*" (my italics) is a timely reminder that the reconciliation of emotion and "scientific objectivity" which the three symposiasts seek, like all men of imaginative good will, need imply no ultimate sacrifice of objectivity. Art and literature have their own fidelity to "things as they are," however hard it may be to give an adequate accounting of what such fidelity demands.

Hampshire warns us against too directly fingering and testing works of the imagination for social and moral relevance. Yet his own essay, like the others,

demonstrates the feasibility, in Frye's words, "of formulating the larger views and perspectives that mark
the cultivated man, and of relating knowledge to the
kind of beliefs and assumptions that unite knowledge
to the good life."

It is a great pleasure to thank all three writers for
their memorable contributions to this important task.

MAX BLACK

Ithaca, New York
January 1967

Contents

NORTHROP FRYE

The Knowledge of Good and Evil

Iɴ the eighteenth century there was some confidence that, in Samuel Johnson's words, no new discoveries were to be made in the field of morality. But new discoveries continued to be made elsewhere, most remarkably in science, and these have had their effect on our conceptions of morality as well. The development of science emphasized the value of the "scientific method," but most expositions of that method turn out to be, not so much methodologies, as statements of a moral attitude. To achieve anything in the sciences, one needs the virtue of detachment or objectivity. One starts out with a tentative goal in mind, but on the way to it one must consider evidence impartially and draw only the strictly rational conclusions from that evidence. Cooking or manipulating the evidence to make it fit a preconceived idea works against detachment. And though we may say that detachment is an intellectual rather than a moral virtue, it becomes increasingly clear as we go on that such a distinction is without meaning. The persistence in keeping the mind in a state of disciplined sanity, the courage in facing results that may deny or contradict everything that one had hoped to achieve—these are obviously moral qualities, if the phrase means anything at all.

The triumphs of these virtues in modern civilization have naturally, and rightly, given them a high place in our scale of values. They are most clearly displayed in the physical sciences, which are so largely informed by mathematics, but as the social sciences developed, they too felt the powerful pull of detachment, and so they became increasingly behavioristic, phenomenological, and restricted to what can be observed and described. At present it may be said that the principle, which is also a moral principle, that every discipline must be as scientific as its subject matter will allow it to be, or abandon all claim to be taken seriously, is now established everywhere in scholarship.

Thus in the general area of the "humanities," history is a subject which can doubtless never be a science, in the sense of being founded on repeatable experiments, informed by mathematics, or leading to prediction. But there is a scientific element involved in the choice of historical evidence which distinguishes history from legend, and prevents, say, a British historian from including Atlantis, Merlin, and King Lear in his purview. Again, if the historian is attempting to set up a system of causation in his history, he will avoid indefinable causes and restrict himself to what he can observe and describe. And while one historian may believe in something incredible to another, such as the resurrection of Jesus or the miracles of a medieval saint, the sense of a predictable order of nature is so strong that the incredulous historian will set the pattern for his colleague. That is, whatever any reasonable and well-disposed historian finds incredible is likely also to be historically unfunctional in the work of another historian who believes it.

Similarly, literary critics are slowly and reluctantly beginning to realize that the evaluative comparison of literary works and traditions gives us no knowledge of literature, but merely rearranges what we already know, or think we know. Whatever gives us knowledge of literature has, like genuine history and genuine philosophy, a detached and objective element in it that distinguishes it from elegant rumination. The hope of developing an axiological science in criticism, as elsewhere, remains so far only a hope. As for religion, its resistance to the same pressure has been long and stubborn, but is visibly collapsing. For long it was felt that the religious mind, like the White Queen in Alice, specialized in believing the impossible. The present tendency to "demythologizing" in religion means, first, that beliefs which are contradicted by the plainest evidence of history or science, such as the quasi-historical fantasies of the Anglo-Israelites or the "fundamentalism" that translates the hymn of creation in Genesis into a textbook of geology, are intellectually wrong. Consequently, because of the way that such beliefs shut doors in the mind and prevent the whole mind from coming into focus on anything, they are in the long run morally wrong as well. In all areas of knowledge we distinguish the observed fact, which depends on sense experience, from the context of the fact, which depends not so much on reason as on a sense of convention about what is, at the time, felt to be reasonable. Truth in religion is increasingly felt to be something that conforms to scientific and scholarly conceptions of truth, instead of being thought to reside primarily in the miraculous, or in the transcendence of other conventions of truth.

Demythologizing is a very inappropriate, not to say foolish, term for what is actually mythologizing, as any withdrawal of religious structures from ontological assertion is bound to transform them into myths. This process has now reached a crucial stage. As the principle of objectivity as the guide to truth continues to make its way, certain types of conceptions, which do not lend themselves to observation, tend to become unusable. What reality can now be attached to the word "God," if it no longer means anything objective? Is it a word that can still be used, like "mind" in psychology or "life" in biology, as a kind of metaphorical signpost, pointing to things that manifest themselves as complexes of observable behavior? If so, what complexes? Or is it a word that depends solely on projection or hypostasis, like such terms as devil, angel, god with a small g, daemon, or (in most contexts) soul, which can only be asserted to exist? It is so fatally easy to name things that are not there: the lion and the unicorn have exactly the same *grammatical* status. Or, finally, is the conception "God," which has never been anything but a nuisance as a scientific hypothesis, simply a dead word, like "ether" in physics, which does not even need a Michelson-Morley experiment to knock it on the head? The case of religion is of particular importance in discussing morality in scholarship, because our traditional morality has been bound up with religion, and religion with belief in the existence of a personal God. In Tourneur's *Atheist's Tragedy* (1611), the word "atheist" also means what we should now mean by a psychopath. Anyone at that time who renounced a personal God would be assumed to have renounced every moral principle as well. Today, most responsible theologians would agree that the statement "There is a God" is of very little religious and no moral significance. It is clear that the conviction we began with, that no new discoveries are to be made in morality, was premature, even if we are still only at the stage of unmaking some of our old discoveries.

In the creative arts the virtues of detachment and objectivity do not, at first sight, seem to apply. The artist is not bound to evidence and rational deduction: he makes a functional use of emotional and even repressed factors in his mental attitude which the scientist as such must sublimate. Yet the cult of objectivity has been very strong in the arts too for over a century, especially in literature. Zola thought of his novels as applied sociology; Flaubert and Joyce recommended an Olympian detachment as the only position worthy of the artist; even the poets insisted that writing poetry was an escape from personality. If any serious contemporary writer were attacked on moral grounds, his defense would almost certainly be based on the moral virtue of detachment. He is trying, he would say, to tell the truth as he sees it, like the scientist. Such a defense would relate to content, but, in form, perhaps the *craftsmanship* of the artist, his effort by reworking and revising to let his creation take its own shape, is what corresponds in the arts to the scientist's objectivity. In the long run, subjective art is as impossible as subjective science, art being also a mode of communication, and the artist's personal emotions have only a typical or representative status in his art.

The permeation of ordinary scholarly life by the same virtue is marked in the deference paid to impersonality. A scholar is supposed not to write or to read an unfavorable review with any personal application; his friendships are not supposed to be affected by theoretical disagreements; students are instructed that "failure" means only not meeting an objective standard, and does not refer to them as human beings. It is significant that the *personal appropriation* of knowledge is not considered the scholar's social goal. The scholar whose social behavior reflects his knowledge too obtrusively is a pedant, and the pedant, whatever the degree of his scholarship, is regarded as imperfectly educated.

Yet there is a widespread popular feeling, expressed

in many clichés, that the pedant, the scholar who does not accurately sense the relation between scholarship and ordinary life, is in fact typical of the university and its social attitude. The forward impetus of the scientific spirit backfires in the public relations department: the disinterested pursuit of knowledge acquires, for its very virtues, the reputation of being unrelated to social realities. The intellectual, it is thought, lives in an over-simplified Euclidean world; his attitude to society is at best aloof, at worst irresponsible; his loyalties and enmities, when they exist, have the naïve ferocity of abstraction, a systematic preference of logical extremes to practical means. A fair proportion of incoming freshmen, in my experience especially women, though mildly curious about the scholarly life, are convinced that it is an "ivory tower," and that only a misfit would get permanently trapped in it. I call this popular view a cliché, which it clearly is, but the clichés of social mythology are social facts. And what this particular cliché points to, rightly or wrongly, is the insufficiency of detachment and objectivity as exclusive moral goals.

The scholarly virtue of detachment, we said, is a moral virtue and not merely an intellectual one: what is intellectual about it is its context. It turns into the vice of indifference as soon as its context becomes social instead of intellectual. Indifference to what? Indifference, let us say, to what we may call, with the existentialists, concern. By concern I mean something which includes the sense of the importance of preserving the integrity of the total human community. Detachment becomes indifference when the scholar ceases to think of himself as participating in the life of society, and of his scholarship as possessing a social context. We see this clearly when we turn from the subject itself to the social use made of it. Psychology is a science, and must be studied with detachment, but it is not a matter of indifference whether it is used for a healing art, or for "motivational research" designed to force people to buy what they neither want nor need, or for propaganda in a police state.

The challenge of concern may come in many forms, and from either a revolutionary or a conservative attitude. Marxism has done much to popularize the view that all social detachment is illusion. On the other hand, Burke laid down a program of pragmatic and short-range concern in opposition to revolutionary tendencies of his time which he described as "metaphysical," a deductive effort to force human destinies into conclusions from large and loose premises about the rights of man. Such conceptualizing of social activity tends to sacrifice the immediate for the distant good: it achieves a detachment from the present situation which is really only indifference to it. The kind of progressivism that says: "If we shoot a hundred thousand farmers now, we may have a more efficient system of collectivized agriculture in the next generation," or: "We need something like a nuclear war if we are to stabilize the population explosion," are examples of the kind of indifference that Burke had in mind.

It is clear that concern and morality are closely connected: morality, in fact, in the sense of the kind of obligation that enables man to preserve his relation to society, is the central expression of concern. What we have to determine is to what extent concern is a scholarly virtue, and whether or not it is, like detachment, a precondition of knowledge. Traditionally, morality has been primarily the safeguarding of the community against all attacks on it. Its ultimate sanction is the giving up of the individual life to preserve the social one, whether in war or in capital punishment. But the safeguarding of the community is not the whole of concern. Concern includes a dialectical value-judgment: the assumption that life is better than death, happiness better than misery, freedom better than slavery, for all men without exception, or significant exception. Human life is socially organized and cannot achieve its goals without such organization, yet any given society may bring death, misery, or slavery on many or even the majority of its members. A man who feels such concern can thus never wholly repudiate nor wholly support his particular society: there must always be a tension between one's loyalties and one's projected desires.

Traditionally, however, what I have called the dialectic of concern has been strictly subordinated to accepting one's own society. In proportion as this is true, society incorporates the dialectic of concern in a class-structure wherein one class derives a greater share of leisure, privilege, and personal liberty from the labor of the rest of society. The same pattern appears in religion (where the concern is "ultimate," as Tillich says), when the division takes the form of heaven and hell, salvation and damnation. As long as the dialectic of concern was assumed to be completed in another world, the class structure of this one could be accepted as a necessary transition to it. To that extent the instinct of Western Europe was sound in regarding Christianity as the palladium of its social structure. A more radical tension has begun to develop since, say, around Rousseau's time. It was probably Rousseau who brought out most vividly the contrast between what civilization demands and what man most profoundly wants. Since then, the reconciling of the dialectic of concern with the social structure has tended to take one of two forms, depending on whether the general-will side or the noble-savage side of Rousseau's thought is stressed. One form, clearest in Marxism, calls for a revolutionary movement from the depressed part of society to put an end to the perversion of concern in the social structure, along with its religious projection. The other, which has taken hold in America, calls for the maintaining of an open society to resist any such revolution, on the ground that it would merely set up a new establishment, and one much harder to dislodge.

The traditional assumption that man can do nothing without a specific social organization takes different forms in our day. One of these is the sense of the futility of individual effort, which in turn leads to a rationalizing of "commitment" or "engagement," that is, attaching oneself to something that looks big and strong enough to get somewhere on its own. The attraction of Communism for many European intellectuals is usually rationalized on this basis. You obviously can't lick them, the argument runs, so you'll have to join them, or their most powerful enemy. Yet the expression of concern seems morally much more clear-cut when it takes the form of a minority resistance movement, like the resistance of the French to the Nazis, of the Hungarians to the Communists, of Negroes to white supremacy, of the Vietcong to the Americans. It is still more so in proportion as the cause appears quixotic, hopeless, futile, or abandoned by others. Those who die for their country in war help to preserve the life of their community in time, but the hopeless cause is invisible, though believed by its martyrs to be present. In religion, an invisible but present heaven may be the guarantee, so to speak, of the reality of the community to which martyrdom bears "witness" (the original sense of martyr). The apocalyptic visions of the Phaedo and the New Testament make the deaths of Socrates and of Christ more intelligible. But even without religion the nonparticipating expression of concern, when carried to the point of death, has an intense moral challenge about it. The self-cremating of Buddhist and American conscientious objectors to the Vietnam war is an example. The Nuremberg and other Nazi trials even raised the question whether a (necessarily hopeless) resistance to the demands of a perverted social order was not only morally but legally binding, and whether one who did not make such a resistance could be considered a criminal. It was feared at the time, no doubt correctly, that the nations who prosecuted these trials would not show enough moral courage to respect this principle where their own interests were involved. In contrast, the more powerful the social structure, the more apt one's loyalty to it is to modulate from concern to concerned indifference. The enemy become, not people to be defeated, but embodiments of an idea to be exterminated.

The real growing point of concern, we have indicated, is not the mere wish that all men should attain liberty, happiness, and more abundant life, nor is it the mere attachment to one's own community: it is rather the sense of the difference between these two things, the perception of the ways in which the human ideal is thwarted and deflected by the human actuality. If there is no moral concern for all humanity, and only concern for one's own society, then concern is reversed into anxiety, which is the vice of concern, as indifference is the vice of detachment. Anxiety in this sense is a negative concern, a clinging to the accustomed features of one's society, usually connected with a fear of something that has been made into a symbol of the weakening of that society. Every social change, even the most obvious improvements, like abolishing slavery or giving votes to women, or the most trifling novelties in fashion, stir up anxieties of this sort. Religion is a particularly fruitful source of such anxieties, which it inherits from the primitive anxiety known as superstition. Those who are not capable of faith have to settle for anxieties instead.

The wider concern based on the preference of life, freedom, and happiness to their opposites is, as we have just called it, a projection of desire. The source of all dangers to social routine, real or fancied, is man's feeling that his desires are not fulfilled by his community. And when we think of the individual man in this way, as a potential disturber of society, we tend increasingly to think of him, not as reasoning man or feeling man, but as sexual man. Eros is the main spokesman for the more abundant life that the social structure fears and resists. When we begin to think along these lines, we soon become aware of the extent to which social anxieties are preoccupied with channeling and sublimating the sexual energies. We begin to understand why certain overt expressions of sexual activity, such as public nakedness or "four-letter words," provide an automatic shock to such anxieties. This familiar Freudian view of anxiety has developed an unexpected social importance in the last decade, when American life has begun to show some contrasting parallels with Communism. The program of Marxism calls for a separation of social loyalty from the ruling class's defense of its privileges, and attaches loyalty to a "proletariat" or group of dispossessed. The contrasting social movements in America have recently taken on a strongly Freudian cast, in which "beat," "hip," and other disaffected groups attempt to define a proletariat in a Freudian sense, as those who withdraw from "square" or bourgeois anxiety-values and form a society of the creative and spontaneous. Associated with them are novelists and poets who emphasize the sexual side of human activity, sometimes with a maundering and tedious iteration. Considered as moralists, such writers are attempting to destroy or at least weaken the anxiety-structure founded on sexual repression.

It is becoming apparent that concern is a normal dimension of everybody, including scholars, and that for scholars in particular it is the corrective to detachment, and prevents detachment from degenerating into indifference. It remains to be seen what its relationship to the learning process is. It seems obvious that concern has nothing directly to do with the content of knowledge, but that it establishes the human context into which the knowledge fits, and to that extent informs it. The language of concern is the language of myth, the total vision of the human situation, human destiny, human aspirations and fears. The mythology of concern reaches us on different levels. On the lowest level is the social mythology acquired from elementary education and from one's surroundings, the steady rain of assumptions and values and popular proverbs and clichés and suggested stock responses that soaks into our early life and is constantly reinforced, in our day, by the mass media. In this country most elementary teaching is, or is closely connected with, the teaching of "the American way of life." A body of social acceptances is thus formed, a myth with a pantheon of gods, some named (Washington, Franklin, Lincoln), others anonymous (the pioneer, the explorer, the merchant adventurer). This body of acceptances gradually evolves into a complete mythology stretching from past golden age to future apocalypse. Pastoral myths (the cottage away from it all, the idyllic simplicity of the world of one's childhood) form at one end of it; stereotypes of progress, the bracing atmosphere of competition, the threat of global disaster, and the hope of preserving this life for one's children form at the other. Such a popular mythology is neither true nor false, neither right nor wrong: the facts of history and social science that it contains are important chiefly for the way in which they illustrate certain beliefs and views. The beliefs and views are primarily about America, but are extended by analogy to the rest of the human race. Such social mythology expresses a concern for society, both immediate and total, which may not be very profound or articulate, but which is a mighty social force for all that. Similar social mythologies have been developed in all nations in all ages: contemporary Americans in fact have an unusually benevolent and well-intentioned one.

Above this is a body of general knowledge, mainly in the area of the humanities, which is also assimilated to a body of beliefs and assumptions. This forms the structure of what might be called initiatory education, the learning of what the cultivated and well-informed people in one's society know, within the common acceptances which give that society its coherence. Initiatory education enters into the university's liberal arts curriculum and is reinforced by the upper strata of the mass media, ranging from churches to the more literary magazines. In our society, the structure of initiatory education is a loose mixture of ideas, beliefs and assumptions, different in composition for each person, but not so different as to preclude communication on its own primarily social level. It forms a body of opinion which I call the mythology of concern. By a myth, in this context, I mean a body of knowledge assimilated to or informed by a general view of the human situation. Some myths in this sense are pure expressions of belief, like the myth of progress. Some are beliefs which are not so much true as going to be made true by a certain program of social action: this is the sense in which Sorel generally uses the word, and it also characterizes the myth of Marxism, according to the *Theses on Feuerbach*.

The traditional picture of scholarship as an intensely specialized activity, motivated by detachment and the pursuit of truth for its own sake, is correct as far as it goes. The arts, and the detailed research which is scholarship in this more restricted sense, emerge out of initiatory education like icebergs, with an upper part which is specialized and a lower part which is submerged in the scholar's general activity as a human being. The mythology of initiatory education is not itself scholarship in the restricted sense, but its upper levels modulate into a scholarly area of great and essential importance. The scholar is involved with this area in three ways: as a teacher, as a popularizer of his own subject, and as an encyclopedist. That is, if he happens to be interested in conspectus or broad synthesizing views, he will spend much or all of his time in articulating and making more coherent his version of his society's myth of concern. A great deal of philosophy (in fact this is often supposed to be philosophy's role), of history, and of social science takes this form. Relatively few such myths are so firmly embedded in the facts as to be actual hypotheses, capable of being definitely proved or disproved; their importance is rather in their effectiveness in extending the reader's perspective. The mythology of concern, taken as a whole, is not a unified body of knowledge, nor is the knowledge it contains always logically deduced from its beliefs and assumptions, nor does one necessarily believe in everything that one accepts from it. But it does possess a unity nonetheless, and those who have most effectively changed the modern world—Rousseau, Marx, and Freud have come up at different times during this discussion—are those who have changed the general pattern of our mythology.

The world of scholarship, in the restricted sense, is too specialized and pluralistic to form any kind of over-all society. What unites the scholars of the "two cultures" is not an interest in one another's field of scholarship, but their common participation in their society, their common stake in that society, their common ability to take part in the dialogue within the mythology of concern. Each scholar, left purely to his own scholarship, would see the human situation only from his own point of view, and the resulting sectarianism would probably destroy society, as the confusion of tongues led to the abandoning of Babel. Hence the importance of having an area of scholarship intermediate between general information and the pursuit of detailed research. It is essentially an activity of exploring the social roots of knowledge, of maintaining communication among scholars, of formulating the larger views and perspectives that mark the cultivated man, and of relating knowledge to the kind of beliefs and assumptions that unite knowledge with the good life.

But it is equally important to recognize where this kind of scholarship is. There is a persistent belief that the unifying of the different fields of scholarship is the final aim of scholarship. But in an open society the unifying of the myth of concern should never be carried to the point of losing the sense of the autonomy of scholarship. A completely unified myth of concern tends to assume that it already has all the important answers, that whatever scholarship has yet to disclose will be either consistent with what is now believed or else wrong, and that it has the right to prescribe the direction in which scholarship is to go. In this situation the myth of concern becomes an anxiety myth. The mythology of the Middle Ages was much more completely unified than ours, so much so as to inspire envy in every age since, down to the revival of Thomism in the last generation. Yet it fought hard for its fictions: the resistance of authority to scholarship did not stop with Galileo, and it is hard to believe that it has stopped now. Marxism is also a myth of concern which has become an anxiety myth when it has been politically established. It interferes less with the autonomy of science than with the arts and humanities, which are more likely to develop rival myths of concern. Its interference with the sciences, for one thing, has usually been disastrous. An extreme example, now officially repudiated, was Lysenko's genetics, whose proponent revived a curious neoscholastic method of arguing, first proving the correct attitude to genetics out of Marx and Lenin, and then asserting that this attitude would be found to fit the facts when the facts were examined. Hysterical right-wing groups in America, working of course mainly on the level of stock response, also attempt to set up a myth of "Americanism" as a criterion for all cultural activity that they get to hear about. When art and scholarship are left autonomous, it is assumed that all unification of knowledge is provisional, and that new discoveries, new ideas, and new shapings of the creative imagination may alter it at any time. The open society thus has an open mythology; the closed society has a controlling myth from which all scholarship is assumed to be logically derived.

One reason why our myth of concern is not as well unified as that of the Middle Ages is that all myths of concern are anthropocentric in perspective, and physical science, at least, refuses to have anything to do with such a perspective. The physical scientist finds his subject less rooted in the myth of concern than the philosopher, the historian, or the theologian. The latter find it more difficult to separate their subjects from their social commitments: they may even find it something of a struggle to preserve intellectual honesty in their arguments, to let facts speak for themselves and avoid twisting them into the directions called for by their commitments. Even in the social sciences detachment and concern may struggle with one another like Jacob with his angel. But the physical scientist's enemy is more likely to be indifference than anxiety, and even a genuine interest in the social context of his scholarship has some unexpected barriers to surmount. Naturally the main outlines of the scientific picture of the world are a part of our general cultural picture, and naturally, too, any broad and important scientific hypothesis, such as evolution or relativity, soon filters down into the myth of concern. But scientific hypotheses enter the myth of concern, not as themselves, but as parallel or translated forms of themselves. An immense number of conceptions in modern thought owe their existence to the biological theory of evolution. But social Darwinism, the conception of progress, the philosophies of Bergson and Shaw, and the like, are not applications of the *same* hypothesis in other fields: they are mythical analogies to that hypothesis. By the time they have worked their way down to stock response, as when slums are built over park land because "you can't stop progress," even the sense of analogy gets a bit hazy. If a closed myth like official Marxism does not interfere with physical science, we have still to remember that physical science is not an integral part of the myth of concern.

We have spoken not merely of scholarship but of the arts also as needing autonomy if society is to preserve its freedom. The reasons why the arts are included belong to another paper, but the role of literature in the myth of concern is relevant here. It is an ancient belief that the original framers of the myth of concern were the poets, acting as "unacknowledged legislators," in Shelley's phrase. In literature the dialectic of concern, the separation of life, freedom, and happiness from their opposites, expresses itself in two tonalities, so to speak: the romantic and the ironic visions. The romantic vision is of the heroic, the pleasurable, the ideal, of that with which one feels impelled to identify oneself. The ironic vision is the vision of the anguished, the nauseated, and the absurd. Besides these, there are the two great narrative movements, the tragic and the comic, which move toward the ironic and romantic cadences respectively.

The ironic vision is the one which is predominant in our day, and its features of anguish, nausea, and absurdity have been deeply entrenched in the contemporary myth of concern. We have noted the importance of detachment in scholarship and its close connection with the scientific method. Science is based on a withdrawal of consciousness from existence, a capacity to turn around and look at one's environment, which is perhaps the most distinctively human of all acts. It is the act that turns the experiencing being into a subject, confronting an objective world from which it has separated itself. The ironic vision is, so to speak, a detachment from detachment: it recognizes the emotional factors of alienation, loneliness, and meaninglessness lurking in the subject-object relationship which the activity of science ignores. The heart of the ironic vision, however, is the vision of the kind of society that such a solitude creates, a society unable to communicate and united only by hatred or mutual contempt. Perhaps the most concentrated form of the ironic vision is what has been called the dystopia, the description of the social hell that man creates for himself on earth, the society of Orwell's *1984*, Koestler's *Darkness at Noon*, Huxley's *Ape and Essence*, Kafka's *In the Penal Colony*, where the individual finds his identity in seeing his own self-hatred reflected in the torment and humiliation of others.

The goal of the romantic vision is less easy to characterize. Although we should expect it to be the opposite of the ironic vision, some form of social heaven or city of God on earth, it is certainly not, at least not in literature, that anxiety-ridden form known as the utopia. It is rather the happy and festive society formed in the final moments of a comedy around the marriage of the hero and heroine, where the "hero" is not, as a rule, an exceptionally brave or strong person, but only a modest and pleasant young man. It is rather the idyllic simplified world of the pastoral, where the hero is a shepherd with no social pretensions, except that he is also a poet and a lover. We notice that what we feel like identifying ourselves with in literature tends to be social rather than purely individual, a festive group rather than an isolated figure. Even the tragic hero who is necessarily isolated by the action—Achilles or Beowulf or Hamlet—seems to regard his heroism not as something that marks him off from others but as something that he has contributed to his society. It is not the characters but the brave deeds of great men that the Homeric heroes wish to emulate. If they die, they look for nothing more for themselves than the batlike existence of a shadow in Hades: their reputation will be their real immortality. It seems a cold and thin immortality, and yet perhaps there is something in this final trust in fame that is more than a "last infirmity," more than the mere wistful pathos it appears to be.

It is becoming clearer that the impulse which creates the mythology of concern and makes it socially effective is a central part of the religious impulse. Religion in this sense may be without a God; certainly it may be without a first cause or controller of the order of nature, but it can never be without the primitive function of *religio*, of binding together a society with the acts and beliefs of a common concern. Such an impulse starts with one's own society, but if it stops there it sets up a cult of state-worship and becomes perverted. We know in our own experience how our mythology of concern works against exclusiveness: all genuine concern recognizes the claims of Negroes to full citizenship, for example. Yet the kind of problem represented by the disabilities of Negroes is much broader in scope, as many suffer from similar disabilities who are not Negroes, and if we make the symbol of colored skin an end in itself, like some of the proponents of "black power," we merely set up a new kind of anxiety. The force that creates the myth of concern drives it onward from the specific society one is in to larger and larger groups, and finally toward assimilating the whole of humanity to the ideal of its dialectic, its concerned feeling that freedom and happiness are better for everyone without exception than their opposites. All national or class loyalties, however instinctive or necessary, are thus in the long run interim or temporary loyalties: the only abiding loyalty is one to mankind as a whole.

If this were the whole story, the myth of concern would end simply in a vague and fuzzy humanitarianism. But in proportion as one's loyalty stretches beyond one's nation to the whole human race, one's concrete and specific human relationships become more obvious. A new kind of society appears in the center of the world, a society which is different for each man, but consists of those whom he can see and touch, those whom he influences and by whom he is influenced: a society, in short, of neighbors. Who is our neighbor? We remember that this question was asked of Jesus, who regarded it as a serious question, and told the story of the Good Samaritan to answer it. And, as the alien figure of the Samaritan, in a parable told to Jews, makes obvious, one's neighbor is not, or not necessarily, a member of the same social or racial or class group as oneself. One's neighbor is the person with whom one has been linked by some kind of creative human act, whether of mercy or charity, as in the parable itself; or by the intellect or the imagination, as with the teacher, scholar, or artist; or by love, whether spiritual or sexual. The society of neighbors, in this sense, is our real society; the society of all men, for whom we feel tolerance and good will rather than love, is in its background.

We have spoken of the religious impulse as one that creates social ties, and that is as far as we can take it here. The universal good will to men which is one logical form of its development is one that could be expressed by statistical formulas, like the greatest happiness of the greatest number. But the sense of a society of neighbors takes us beyond ethics and values into the question of identity. It would perhaps be a reasonable characterization of religion to say that a man's religion is revealed by that with which he is trying to identify himself.

Throughout civilization there runs a tendency known in the Orient as "making oneself small," of being modest and deprecating about one's own abilities, and being much more ready to concede the abilities of others. Some of this is self-protective hypocrisy, but not all of it is. When we think about our own identity, we tend at first to think of it as something buried beneath what everyone else sees, something that only we can reach in our most solitary moments. But perhaps, for ordinary purposes at least, we may be looking for our identity in the wrong direction. To identify something is first of all to put it in the category of things to which it belongs: the first step in identity is the realization *humanus sum*. We belong to something before we are anything, nor does growing in being diminish the link of belonging. Granted a reasonably well-disposed and unenvious community, perhaps our reputation and influence, what others are willing to think that we are, comes nearer to being our real selves than anything stowed away inside us. In the imagery of Blake's lyric, one may be more genuinely a "clod," something attached to the rest of the earth, than a separated "pebble." In an ideal community there would be no alienation, in the sense used in Marx's early writings: that is, one's contribution to one's community would not be embezzled, used by others at one's expense. In such a community perhaps we could understand more clearly why even the tragic heroes of literature attempt to identify themselves with what they are remembered for having done. In the society that the mythology of concern ultimately visualizes, a man's real self would consist primarily of what he creates and of what he offers. The scholar as man has all the moral dilemmas and confusions of other men, perhaps intensified by the particular kind of awareness that his calling gives him. But *qua* scholar what he is is what he offers to his society, which is his scholarship. If he understands both the worth of the gift and the worth of what it is given for, he needs, so far as he is a scholar, no other moral guide.

STUART HAMPSHIRE

Commitment and Imagination

I SHALL accept without qualification the terms in which Professor Northrop Frye states the opposition which is to underlie our whole discussion. He states this opposition as one of life, freedom, and happiness against death, slavery, and anguish. These words do for me define the oppositions of morality closely enough. I am ready to agree that the contribution that humanistic scholarship makes must be explained within the setting of such an opposition. Scholarship can claim no final autonomy; that is, the principles that are to guide its direction are not self-justifying, obvious, or beyond question. We need to see why humanistic scholarship must be preserved. What unavoidable needs does it serve? Under what conditions has it lost its way? What costs ought we be prepared to pay to preserve it? Within what limits, and how, does it sustain and extend freedom, and maintain an indispensable enjoyment? It is clear that scholarship has to be defended against encroachments and diver-

31

sions, if it is to survive. There could well be societies and nations, highly developed intellectually and in many respects progressive, from which humanistic scholarship had largely disappeared, or in which it was allowed only a very minor place. Why do we want to defend it against these diversions, the diversions, for example, of the higher journalism? Or against the diversion of intellect to public rhetoric and the justification of public policy? Or, more threatening still, against the subordination of scholarship, and of the free play of criticism, to the needs of social betterment—to that Leviathan, now usually called Society, which is often conceived as some giant boarding school, in which we are all required to prove ourselves as of sound character?

I ought to explain that I shall include, under the heading of "humanistic scholarship," the exact study of history in all its many forms, including the history of thought, the study of literature, of the arts, of particular languages and language in general, and of philosophy. I shall also make reference to original, freely imaginative writing, which is not scholarship at all, in order to keep our discussion open.

I wish to follow a slightly different order of argument from Professor Frye's. For reasons that I hope gradually to make clear, I want to put more stress on the needs of the individual and less stress on the social order than does Professor Frye. I think that we shall in effect be discussing the conditions under which human beings are likely to remain independent adults, and at the same time sane, not anxious, distracted, or emotionally numb. This theme is suggested to me by Professor Frye himself, when he distinguishes the different virtues, detachment and concern, and their corresponding defects, indifference and anxiety. It is more than a verbal point that concern is ordinarily taken to be an emotional interest in something, which is distinguished among emotional interests by being a slowly developed, adult and reflective emotion; concern is not just any gust of sympathetic feeling. So Hume thought of concern for humanity, and this is the sense that some psychologists have attached to the word. As an emotion, or an emotional attitude, it involves the least possible projection of the subject's own disconnected fantasies and wishes. A certain degree of "abstraction from the contingent interests of the subject," in Kant's words, is constitutive of concern. Anxiety, by contrast, is the almost-technical name of an emotional turbulence which has its source in an inner conflict and not in the commonly recognized properties of those external things and persons with which it becomes associated. We project our inner anxiety on to situations, in the sense that if we describe the subject's interest or state as one of anxiety, we imply that the inner turbulence will not greatly vary with the varying properties of things and persons around him. But concern is always concern for an object recognized as independent, and it entails a concentrated attention and interest, and not a distracted and varying one. The emotion, and the drives associated with it, depend primarily for their

33

strength upon beliefs about the object of concern: beliefs, not wishes or fantasies. It seems to me right to treat these terms, even in our unscientific discussion, as carrying some of the theoretical connotations with which they have been endowed in clinical psychology. We can only understand the distinction between concern and anxiety if we recall this theoretical background.

Professor Frye himself speaks of the controlled withdrawal from an emotional engagement with reality, and of the detachment of the subject, which is a necessary preliminary to any scientific exploration of reality. So he is using the terms of individual psychology. I shall happily continue along this path and forget for the moment morality as the condition of orderly life in society. Morality can also be considered as the individual's own defense against, and control of, his original, and now often unfitting, instincts, and of the primary emotions and impulses derived from them. The withdrawal from reality which Professor Frye mentions is only the extreme and final form of a withdrawal of subjective feeling from external objects, which is required even for the more elementary control and manipulation of the environment. It is the condition of maturity not to experience things and persons simply as hostile or friendly, as satisfying or frustrating our desires, and as having an aspect and an expression that is felt to be either comforting or alarming; rather in maturity one has to experience objects as utterly independent and needing to be explored, and as having principles of motion of their own. Let us assume that this growing up to maturity takes place gradually, in the setting of family relationships, and that earlier stages in the process leave their effects in the mind, like a sediment or silt, on which the imagination subsequently feeds and from which it grows. Detached curiosity, the exploratory attitude, is a condition not only of scientific investigation but also of the free exercise of the imagination. As science comes to be distinguished, during the growing-up process, from magic, so imagination comes to be distinguished from fantasy, interpreted as a direct expression of wish. Professor Frye implies that it is the condition of any kind of art, which can be of some lasting interest, that it should not be a direct expression of a private pathology, or the projection of a private world of fantasy. The projection of wish and fantasy upon unresisting material is a normal characterization of bad art, or of non-art; whatever else art is, it is certainly the contrary of self-expression in this sense. Neither a novel, nor a poem, nor a work of history, philosophy, or literary criticism is to be valued, either by its author or by its public, for its sincerity and its revelation of the private world of the author. The only sincerity that is, in the long run, tolerable in art is a sincerity that is the unintended by-product of contrivance and of disguise: the kind of sincerity that Stendhal both aimed at and achieved. Sincerity cannot replace imagination and exactness in scholarship. Nor does he who comes to a work of art or literature, as spectator or reader, properly look for a vehicle in which to put his own emotions, fantasies, and wishes.

This process of growing up, and of stripping objects of their expressive properties, as one learns to explore and manipulate them, incurs a large psychological cost; and this cost is multiplied as one acquires the scientist's respect for the independent laws of change in the environment. The price of full rationality is a separation of argument, and of systematic understanding, from the primary emotions—that is, the emotions that mark gratification or frustration of the instincts; and also the separation of argument and systematic understanding from the more developed emotions that are acquired in the growing-up process itself. Particularly in learning to be rational in our attitude to other persons, and therefore in learning to understand their behavior as independent of our desires, we learn to disconnect our own emotions from their immediate and natural expression in behavior. By this art of inhibition and concealment, we acquire an inner life of hoarded feeling. These feelings we are now ready to bestow upon fitting objects, under appropriate safeguards; so we are ready for vicarious experience in the enjoyment of art and fiction, and of imitation generally, and we develop the vocabulary that is needed for this control. We come to speak, and to think, of our own emotions, now held apart from immediate expression, as though they were objects which we can observe and explore; and because we can observe them, we may also control them. The problem then is to reintroduce these controlled emotions into the world of objects, to find objective correlates for them, which will finally give form and substance to feelings that might otherwise be inchoate and confused. The withdrawn emotions have to be bestowed upon objects through appropriately contrived channels. We have learnt to interpret the physiognomy of people, their expression and movements, as signs from which we can infer their inner states and so anticipate their conduct. For we rightly think of our own direct emotional responses as interfering with detached observation, as preventing us from seeing the truth about objects in the external world, and particularly the truth about persons. If we are to be successful in manipulating people, as we must be, we will naturally develop a technology of social manipulation, and look to scientific method to help us. So we shall look for general laws of behavior and become accustomed to dealing with people as instances of types. Thus we subtract what might be called the tertiary properties of objects: that is, their expressive, aesthetically interesting, physiognomic properties, in the interest of a more precise manipulation. We shall look to the human sciences—to psychology, sociology, linguistics, social anthropology—for the basic structure, the underlying mechanism of human behavior; and in this context we will need to disregard the distracting surface properties of behavior.

The first and now classical defense of a humanistic education, and of the role of the scholar and critic, comes from Kant and Schiller—the Schiller of *Letters on an Aesthetic Education*—namely, that it is a condition of a restored wholeness of mind that there should be an exploration of reality which concentrates upon the surface properties of things and of persons, to compensate for the scientific exploration of the basic structure, of the mechanism of causality, governing external objects. Having stripped persons, languages, and things of their surface and sensuous qualities for the sake of scientific understanding, we shall try to restore interest in these properties, a free interest, through the visual arts, through fiction and poetry; turning away from psychology or sociology with their necessary interest in structure, we shall look to history, with its necessary interest in the particular case. We will look to the external world to find what visual forms, what patterns of sound, arrangements of words and images, what stories, will sustain the weight of the emotional energy that we have displaced from its natural and immediate expression. We will insist that we understand the appropriateness of some works as the objective correlates of emotion; for these works will be one of the principal ways left to us of identifying and describing the emotions themselves, once they have been disconnected from action and have become parts of the inner world. We will then be able to communicate with other men about the inner world through these objective embodiments of feeling, which can be objects of common perceptions and can elicit a common understanding and response.

In the *Critique of Judgment* Kant had characterized

this necessity of an aesthetic education as the necessity of the free play of the imagination, having first carefully distinguished imagination from subjective wish. Men may communicate with each other, and reach agreement upon judgments of taste, across all other differences between them, just because in aesthetic judgment they are appealing to their common imaginative perceptions. The tertiary properties, aesthetic and physiognomic, which the free imagination finds in works of literature, music, or the visual arts, are really there to be found, at least for a transcendental idealist. But no rules or rational methods can be given for their detection; for the imagination does not deal in concepts and therefore does not deal in rules. So Kant created the contrast between the imagination, as on the one hand opposed to private fantasy and on the other to scientific intellect. Its proper object is to be found in the surface qualities of things and in the immediately perceived style and manner of a performance. Its use, however, is a genuine exploration of the external world, and not just the discovery of personally gratifying features within it. This conception of imagination has provided the most convincing philosophical foundation, known to me, for the distinct claims of humanistic scholarship. It is a philosophical justification, and does not draw, or pretend to draw, upon individual psychology as a science. But it fits such little psychological data as we possess.

But you will ask what the relevance is of this Kantian conception of the imagination to the specific problems of a scholar's commitment. First, one must get rid of a possible misunderstanding; it is plain that the same unconditional requirement of accuracy and truthfulness is imposed on humanistic scholarship (historical, linguistic, critical, philosophical) as upon any investigation in the natural and social sciences. The first condition of scholarship of any kind is an unqualified respect for evidence, for the complexity of the objects and evidence under study. The scholar and the natural scientist are equally committed to patience, skepticism, slowness, to minute attention to detail, and to the usual disappointment of large designs. The scholar is no less subject to the division of labor under modern conditions than is the natural scientist. He can only expect to know, or really to know, to establish finally and accurately, very little of that which he first thought might be known. But this requirement becomes binding only after a question has been asked, after a problem has been raised, and a path of investigation marked out. The really difficult issue of commitment, and of the morality of scholarship, is this: how are we to decide what questions are worth asking, what problems are worth raising, or, more strongly, what problems must be raised? Once the problems have been picked out as worthy of prolonged research and attention, nothing but the scruples of accuracy and completeness, as far as the subject matter permits, is relevant. In the selection of problems or areas of research—as pressing and serious, or as needed or necessary—commitment is in question. We have to presume that scholarship is not merely defensive, a distraction from our first-order concerns, and in this sense detached.

I think that most really illuminating and permanently interesting scholarship has had as its underlying, and usually unconscious, motive an emotional conflict that is particularly felt as a conflict by the scholar himself; it is a conflict that engages his imagination and does not remain as a direct projection of his own inner feelings. I shall take just one example, not from my own field. The historian Lewis Namier illustrated the commitment of scholarship in our time, as Gibbon and Macaulay in earlier periods, although his achievements as a historian were much more fragmentary. The problems of nationalism, of the functioning of a hereditary aristocracy in government, and of the nature of the British political tradition—all these were, for deep reasons of personal history, first-order concerns of his. Therefore in writing history he was, at the same time, trying to externalize, and so to understand better, the conflicts which had been decisive in his personal life and in his own political activities. His political activities, no less than his scholarship, centered upon the principle of nationality, upon the idea of a historical community, an idea which he considered that liberals, and progressive thinkers generally, had misunderstood and underrated. He was a committed writer, and indeed teacher, in the sense that his theoretical and practical activities had a traceable common base in deeply felt personal needs. So the reader feels the energy of an exploratory imagination, and a vision that holds together the facts, in all his most characteristic writing. The reader feels that Namier originally needed to get the historical record on these to him essential topics right, even while he also perceives a countervailing need to respect the complexities of the evidence, of the resisting material. This is the tension that makes worth-while scholarship. It would not be difficult to quote other examples—from the sphere of classical philosophy, say, or of literary criticism—to illustrate commitment in this sense. For some great scholars, an imaginative vision of the classical world, which is in intention entirely truthful, and which is in any case controlled by the utmost respect for the complexities of the evidence, has been an outcome of some conflict over Christianity and over its pervasiveness in their up-bringing. Some of the energy in their work comes from this necessary vision of a contrasting ideal—necessary, that is, to them; but this vision is still held in control by respect for objective fact. I think the same point could be illustrated from modern Renaissance studies in the history of art from Burckhardt onward. The commitment, or engagement, I am here speaking of is a contrary of scholarship for scholarship's sake, and of learning for learning's sake; but of course it is not commitment, or engagement, interpreted as a single-minded propagation of a political or moral cause, or of a *Tendenz*. The vitality of scholarship comes precisely from the lack of single-mindedness. It comes from the exploration, conducted in the spirit of objectivity, upon resisting, complex material, of an unrelieved concern, from an urge to find a definite solution, combined with the recognition that definite solutions are scarcely at all to be found in the area of humanistic scholarship. The mistake of many sociologists, and of most Marxist writers, it seems to me, has been to confuse commitment, in the sense of imaginative involvement, with single-mindedness; to move from the proposition that worth-while scholarship, in the last analysis, has as its underlying motive a controlled exploration of moral and emotional conflicts, to the proposition that scholarship ought generally to issue in some advocacy of a program of action, or in the illustration of some independently established social ideal. This is to put the will in the place of the imagination. Following this last sense of commitment, critics sometimes give us a crude selection of heroes of thought and of literature: as if all literature should aspire to the condition of Brecht plays, or all painting to the virtues of Courbet, Léger, or Diego Rivera.

The underlying mistake, I think, is the misconception of the imagination as aimed at unambiguous assertions and at the solution of independently statable problems. As Lukács, with all his often remarked faults, saw, a more many-sided, and therefore permanently interesting, exploration of moral and social conflicts may be found in writers, who, judged by their assertions, were altogether reactionary (Scott, Balzac) than in writers who were, judged by their assertions, enlightened (Anatole France, Zola). It is by now a commonplace that, from Flaubert onward, a high proportion of great European writers have been altogether out of sympathy, in their conscious thinking, with the progressive political movements of their time and with the liberal ideas that have prevailed in the minds of most of their readers. Yet one may well think that more can be learned, more understanding gained, of the emotional and social conflicts of the age, from Eliot, Lawrence, Yeats, Kafka, even from Joyce, than from, say, Brecht or Sartre.

I suspect that this is equally true if we turn to the past, to a historical study of either literature or painting. Those who, we can now see, constitute the center of the permanently interesting work of their time are often those who were resisting, at the conscious level, the advanced thought of their time. I am suggesting that it is of the nature of imagination that it generally deals in conflicts and contradictions, in dubious meanings, and not in definite conclusions and in unambiguous assertions. The energy in any imaginative work comes from that destruction of single-mindedness which allows different interpretations at different levels. This ambiguity, and this absence of reliable tendency, was a principal ground of Plato's banishment of the poets and of his plea for censorship; this, and the fact that the imagination of the poet, musician, or painter plays upon the surface of things, and is unconcerned with their underlying rational structure. Of course I am not denying that great works of literature, and very distinguished works of literary and historical scholarship, have advocated a cause, political, moral or religious, or that such works have often been didactic, and have been in intention works of propaganda, conveying very definite assertions. But I am suggesting that it is not usually their arguments, or their advocacy, which has principally sustained our interest in them. For this interest is shared by those who reject their arguments, and who have seen their advocacy as a mere scaffolding around which the imagination has built. I readily admit that there is a complex question here, which has been raised again by Mr. Empson in writing about Milton, and by Mr. O'Brien in writing about Yeats; it is the question of the relation between belief and the enjoyment of literature, and it goes back at least to Eliot's "The Sacred Wood."

Permit me to illustrate my point about commitment from my own field. Among philosophers in our time, in France no less than in the English-speaking countries, there has been an evident concern centering upon the majestic, highly plausible, claim that the natural sciences will, in the long run, provide the only adequate explanation of the workings of the human mind; that our present domesticated speech about motives and character, virtue and vice, and about the unconscious mind itself, will turn out to be a mere holding operation, a temporary framework, which subsequent generations will view with patronizing indulgence, as we now look back to alchemy with patronizing indulgence: it was a useful beginning, but everything that was not mere error is now safely absorbed in chemistry. So it will be when we have an adequate psychology: this is the claim and not an implausible one. This concern, which evidently goes back to Kant, has once again animated the many contemporary discussions of the philosophy of mind, which do not directly allude to it. In thinkers as dissimilar in method and purpose as Sartre and Wittgenstein, one can clearly detect this concern, together with the suspicion that philosophy itself may now have become a rearguard action against the encroaching claims of scientific explanation, and of the scientific definition of reality. This concern is most subtly expressed in the writings of Wittgenstein, who is the obvious case of the committed philosopher; committed, in the sense that his reader always feels that Wittgenstein is urgently working out in his writings a deep division and conflict which, from his earliest years, had directly involved his emotions, his chosen manner of life, and his sense of the moral and political ills of his time. We can therefore no longer have the illusion that the philosophy of mind, even in its most careful, patient and strictly analytical forms, expresses only an impersonal concern for clear thinking.

The significance of a writer, whether poet or philosopher or historian, and that which makes him worthy of study now, commonly does not reside principally in the conscious intentions behind his work, but rather in the precise nature, as we can now see it, of the conflicts and the imaginative inconsistencies in his work. Perhaps you will allow a rash generalization: any form of civilized life is sustained at the cost of some denial, or reversal, of feeling, and of some self-deception, at the cost of fabricating myths and speculative hypotheses, which will seem, to an entirely detached and scientific eye at some later date, a kind of madness, or at least an indulgence in illusion. Looking back to the philosophy of even thirty years ago, one may think that many of the intense preoccupations of that time were obsessional, unnecessary, a turning away from common sense, or a gratuitous pursuit of academic quibbles. Now perhaps we have emerged into the light of a commonsense understanding of our language. But one can also wonder which of our present discussions in the philosophy of mind will appear obsessional, an unnecessary diversion, in fifty years time. For a certain type of historical consciousness, for example, that of Voltaire, Gibbon, and Hume, and of the eighteenth-century Enlightenment generally, the obsessions and the illusions which have formed civilization in the past were interesting, just because these thinkers believed that they themselves, and their contemporaries, were successfully struggling to be free from illusion: not just from those past illusions, but from all illusions. They really had a vision of the childhood of humanity, and of metaphysical obsessions, as finally in the past; at last it would be possible to live without the illusions, and without the myths and rituals, which had hitherto constituted civilized living. They described this freedom from illusion, this new maturity of mankind, as a living and thinking and writing according to nature, without the accretions of the imagination, which fabricates myths and rituals, both to express and to relieve

47

anxiety. The kind of knowledge required for living and thinking and writing in the open air of nature was taken to be the kind of knowledge which the natural sciences provide: that is, knowledge of the underlying structure, the laws of motion, of psychology as of physics.

But this type of historical consciousness, it was soon seen, and conspicuously seen by Hegel, generated its own characteristic myths, rituals, and symbols. The myths and symbols of the Enlightenment were principally drawn from the pagan world, and they merely replaced the symbolism of Christianity. In their style of language, and in their manner, the writers of the Enlightenment seemed, from the standpoint of succeeding generations, to represent just one temporary set of social conditions, and one type of imagination of the future. Their rhetoric, and their visions, soon seemed as agreeably dated as the furniture and architecture which surrounded them. So Sainte-Beuve, Carl Becker, and many others could make their thought and their literature, which to them had seemed merely natural, a period piece. Their imagination, though strongly denied, had been at work once again in creating an original anthropology.

The conclusion that I would draw, but that I cannot of course prove, is that the claim to an entirely independent, rational, standpoint as a critic of the past, of philosophy, of literature, and of social institutions, is, and always will be, in large part an illusion. A truly detached historical consciousness is not a real possibility. I am myself particularly attracted to thinkers who make this haughty and illusory claim to detachment from the emotional conflicts expressed in their work, and to a Godlike position of surveying nature, and particularly human nature, from a superior, detached, and uncommitted standpoint. Spinoza and Freud are evident examples of this type of imagination, with a similar style, and with a similar claim to absolute detachment and objectivity. But there is a law of opposites at work here; their individual style and their personal history appear only the more strongly in their work. In writing about Spinoza, I could not deceive myself that I had interpreted him from a point of view that would disguise my own concerns with philosophical conflicts of this time which had, and still have for me, emotional overtones. I could only hope that these concerns, and the personal conflicts from which they arose, were representative enough, and that they might bring to attention features of Spinoza's thought which would stir the imagination of others. It was so very obvious that contemporary French writers found in Spinoza the criticism of Cartesian rationalism which they needed to find, and that the great scholar H. A. Wolfson found in Spinoza principally a variation upon the Jewish tradition that descends from Philo. Every interesting commentator betrayed his own commitment. But Spinoza himself did not see, and within his own premises could not have seen, his work as falling within any limited framework; nor would he have admitted that his imagination, fed by the special circumstances

49

of his relation to Judaism and to his ancestors, had contributed anything of substance to his theory of existence, or to his theory of the emotions and of freedom. The geometrical style was designed as a strong denial of any such suggestion, and was a rather too emphatic defense against the suggestion. The imagination is eliminated from his account of true enlightenment; precisely this struggle to achieve an entire detachment, and to describe a moral concern that is unstained by any emotion traceable to an origin in personal history, remains the principal interest of his philosophy. I am of course implying that the struggle was not successful, and could not have been successful.

I am not saying simply that there is an ineliminable personal component, a factor of temperament, in any work in the field of the humanities. For I am assuming that the imagination, which is a faculty of the exploration of reality, and which produces ideas to be tested, either in an art or in an inquiry, is to be distinguished from mere temperament. My suggestion is rather that committed writing, and committed scholarship in the humanities, is always an imaginative working out of problems that are felt to be urgent, in some external, resisting material. The concern ultimately has its roots in an individual history, but the problem has been displaced and given an objective form. The energy comes from the subjective side, but the problems are worked out with strict objectivity in a new material. I have dwelt so continuously on the imagination because of the danger that we should exaggerate the part that conscious intention should play in the deliberate planning of the work: as if a scholar or writer ought to be clear in his own mind that his work has a contemporary social relevance, if he is not to be irresponsible. I doubt whether this is how the imagination works, or can work, whether in literature, history, or philosophy. It is generally only in retrospect that we can see why a concern that might at the time have seemed marginal, scholastic, academic in the abusive sense of this word, was in fact a working out in apparently alien, or even trivial, material of an exemplary conflict of values, which had a much wider relevance. There is a law of indirection here: no doubt some literary critics in England have been in a sense right when they claim that we properly come to literature with ultimate questions about what men are to live for, and that serious criticism should invoke these questions. But, I would add, not directly or head-on. When these questions are too directly raised, and when works of the imagination are fingered and tested for directly evident social and moral relevance, we get disastrous dismissals and misunderstandings, and a narrowing of the opening for new possibilities. Apart from certain English critics, whom I will not name, one need only think of Wells on James, or Gide's commenting on Proust's novel after a first reading, when he took the work to be a mere society novel, or of Sainte-Beuve on Stendhal. For the very opposite principle of criticism, that of looking for the imaginative core of the work, one might take Edmund Wilson's essays on Kipling or Housman—indeed almost any of his literary essays.

Apart from a historical retrospect, we can all, I believe, illustrate from our own experience, however comparatively unimaginative the work, that law of displacement which has led us to translate a deeply felt conflict into a preoccupation, sometimes almost an obsession, with some apparently minor detail of inquiry, whether in philosophy or in criticism or in historical study. It may be a condition of the success of the displacement, of the transference of emotional energy, that we cannot perceive the mechanism at work in us at the time. The law of displacement seems one of the fundamental laws of the imagination. Consider a fairly clear case, the evidence of Henry James's *Notebooks*. A fragment of an anecdote, a name with a description attached, overheard at a dinner party, starts in his mind the imagination of a dramatic situation; the insignificant detail of the particular case will be the starting point, because it seems to carry with it the suggestion of something general, of a modern "type," as he might call it. James knew that he could not tell why the excitement arose in his mind and why just this detail set his imagination to work and carried with it an emotional charge. But looking to the work that emerges, it is sometimes possible for the present-day critic, who has the final body of James's work in front of him, to see the significance and the connection, both the Jamesian conflict and the wider relevance of the story. For the critic or inquiring reader is finding his way back toward the complex sources of the work, unraveling the skein, as well as enjoying the knotted whole: but the author is looking only forward to the next step and to the completion. Therefore one is struck, in reading the notebooks of even this most self-conscious writer, by the gap between the relative triviality, as it often seems, of James's own conscious motives in planning his story, and the much greater complexity and, as it now seems, wider relevance of the story itself. Hence the old maxim "trust the tale and not the teller" applies. Certainly my contemporaries at Oxford in the 1930's found in *The Golden Bowl* a wonderful portrayal of the relations between European corruption, or civilization, and a contrasting corruption, or civilization, of two kinds of appetite, and two kinds of cunning. This was a portrayal that was in part consciously intended, but that was, in its most permanently interesting features, also unintended, a discovery made by James's imagination, fed by its own unconscious sources. No direct, planned confrontation of this topic, which is only one of the many sources of interest in the novel, could be expected to reach such richness of suggestion and many-sidedness.

Certainly in philosophy the many recent calls to beware of the ivory tower, and of the new scholasticism, and to return to the pressing topics of public discussion, seem to me to have been quite misguided. The law of displacement is certainly at work in philosophy. The traditional problems are often better approached obliquely, piecemeal, and in disguised forms. One cannot tell when some apparently disconnected advance in the philosophy of language, in linguistic theory itself, or in logic, will transform a traditional problem which has been left untouched by direct assault. Looking back, I think I could now fit the very elaborate discussions of phenomenalism before the war, at the time apparently so academic and remote from common concerns, into their place, a necessary place, in the history of thought. Again, the apparently academic accumulations of dictionary facts associated with the name of J. L. Austin have a significance of which their author was not fully conscious when he began his inquiries. Everyone will be able to think of examples of apparently disproportionate demands for accuracy and detail in academic controversies which in their day had no discernible links to the pressing social and moral issues of that time. There were many of us who before the war felt strongly committed to apparently disconnected problems of the most academic kind in the theory of knowledge, and who were at the same time equally committed to political causes. Superficially, there seemed no connection between the epistemology and the issue of what kind of socialism might be practicable. I am inclined to think now, thirty years later, that I can discern some of the connecting lines of relevance—certainly very wavy, unstraight lines—that lead from the intricacies of the sense-datum controversy through issues in the philosophy of mind, which

54

are themselves indirectly linked to definitions of freedom, and so to political programs.

My conclusion therefore on this issue of commitment is twofold. First, one cannot hope, and must not try, to direct research in the humanities principally by rational calculation of directly useful and socially relevant results; one must not crudely apply the criterion, "Is this work now relevant to already recognized social needs?" Imaginative energy has largely incalculable sources and serves largely unconscious needs. The only safe criterion is the degree of intellectual excitement that a work or a problem—in, say, philosophy or literary criticism—provokes, and the degree of exactness and care which men are ready to bring to its exploration. Why they are ready for so much concern may not be understood for many years. Secondly, we do well not to deceive ourselves with claims to absolute detachment, and not to be ashamed of the largely unconscious roots of our commitments to particular inquiries. Perhaps we shall never be able to explain how these inquiries fit into a total scheme of needed knowledge. To put it paradoxically: in this field one should do, as a matter of policy, what one strongly feels that one must do, without any policy at all.

CONOR CRUISE O'BRIEN

Politics and the Morality of Scholarship

U s i n g language taken from Rousseau, Robespierre's Committee of Public Safety divided humanity into *les purs* and *les corrompus*. The pure were authorized to put to death the corrupt, those who were incurably infected by irrational institutions. In our day Mao Tse-tung, Robespierre's successor as puritan revolutionary leader, has made a similar judgment about literature:

Then does not Marxism destroy the creative mood? Yes, it does. It definitely destroys creative moods that are feudal, petty-bourgeois, liberalistic, individualistic, nihilistic, art-for-art's sake, aristocratic, decadent, or pessimistic, and every other creative mood that is alien to the masses of the people and to the proletariat.[1]

That the literal application of Mao's doctrine would obliterate literature and literary studies is obvious. To say so, however, is not to refute Mao. For Mao, as for

[1] "Talks at the Yenan Forum on Literature and Art" (1942).

Lenin, revolution—the destruction of an intolerable social order, and the construction of a better one—is the supreme need of our time. Art, literature, scholarship—all activities of privileged minorities—must be subordinated to the general good of humanity, expressed in revolution, consolidation and defense of revolutionary gains, and preparation for further revolution. By this subordination the writer must become a propagandist, the literary critic a critic of propaganda, although his duties in that respect will include demanding what are called "higher artistic standards." The writer must be prepared to do less than his best work if, as is often the case, the second-rate or third-rate would be more helpful to the cause. The critic must be prepared to praise the second-rate or third-rate extravagantly and to denounce the first-rate, if its manifestations seem unhelpful to the interests of the revolution, as these are for the moment assessed by the political leadership. As even those writers who enthusiastically support the idea of subordination to revolution—like Mayakovsky—often prove refractory or injudicious in practice, the critic tends to become the ideological superior and discipliner of the creative writer and to occupy a place of considerable significance in the political hierarchy. As in Chernyshevsky's day, under the Czardom, so today what is formally literary criticism may be in substance political debate. Today, as distinct from Chernyshevsky's day, it is likely to be a debate on behalf of different sections of those who hold power. The writer criticized may well be a scapegoat for ideological sins completely unknown to him; he could also become a praised prize-winner in a game whose changing rules he never understood.

Under conditions of general revolutionary subordination, the morality of scholarship—in the narrow sense of scientific and professional ethics—is also subject to encroachment. The historian may have to distort or suppress certain events—like the activities of Trotsky in the Revolution—the economist certain figures—as in the early Five-Year Plans—if the interests of the revolution seem to require it. The fact that such pressures and encroachments tend on the whole, though with frequent and serious setbacks, to diminish in the Soviet Union does nothing to alter the principle. The defense and consolidation of revolutionary achievements, the matters that now principally concern the Soviet Union, may not only permit but actually require, at a given moment, relaxation of political discipline in certain spheres, especially in the scientific sphere. Relaxation in such circumstances is not a breach of the subordination principle; it is an application of that principle.

Scholars and artists are likely to reprobate both the theory and practice of revolutionary subordination. We might do well, however, to consider also how our reprobation must look to those whose theory and practice we reprobate. If we say that we cannot accept the need for revolutionary subordination, they can reply that the reason for this is obvious: that since we belong among the principal beneficiaries of the social *status quo* in the world, our assertion of higher values is just a way of expressing, in the language of our mandarin caste, an economically based antagonism. It would not be very easy to refute this. One reason why the doctrine of revolutinary subordination is likely to seem so repulsive to most of us is that most of us do not conceive of revolution as being desirable at all, and therefore a fortiori we cannot conceive of its being worth great moral, intellectual, and other sacrifices. We belong to a comfortable stratum in a country in which the majority of people are also comfortable. Few of us have known conditions such as those that created, in China, the conviction, more strongly held among intellectuals than even among others, that revolution was worth any sacrifice—one's own life, one's family, one's artistic or professional integrity. Most of us are not, I take it, prepared to sacrifice any of these things in this cause, and in the case of artistic and professional integrity we either deplore or condemn the sacrifice. It is well to be sure which we are doing. If we condemn, it is a moral stance implying that we know that no social or political objective can ever justify the slightest departure from artistic or professional integrity. This in turn would imply that even if we knew that by praising a bad novel we could save the lives of some children, we would remain morally obliged to knock the novel and let the children die. If we turn professional ethics into an absolute, which cannot in any circumstances be subordinated to any other values, we are forced I think to approve the incorruptible, infanticidal book reviewer. If we do so, we turn ourselves into callous and posturing pedants, inverted images of Robespierre. If on the other hand we adopt a more pragmatic attitude, and say that mendacious book reviews do not in fact save the lives of children, then the debate shifts from the ground of pure morality to that of the assessment of factual situations. The revolutionary, if we can assume him to have adequate reasons to be candid, might well declare that the right kind of bad novel or bad poem can strengthen the revolutionary will to fight: that the exposure of the badness of such works can weaken such will and lead to revolutionary defeats—for example, to restoration of landlordism in a province, with all the conditions that go with it, including starvation among the children of peasants. And if all these factual, and not implausible, assertions are true, then an honest book review can indeed in certain circumstances kill children. So that if, while rejecting the inverted Robespierre role, we also reject the revolutionary view of the critic's role, we must do so not on grounds of pure morality, but because we think the connection is not proven, and that all that the reasoning will *certainly* result in is a spate of mendacity; in short, the children may or may not be saved, but they will certainly be systematically misinformed.

A stereotyped reply from the revolutionary side to such objections is that in time of war the capitalist world itself, including its intellectuals, accepts the need for a vigorous propaganda effort, necessarily involving a considerable element of distortion and dishonesty.

Even literary scholarship and aesthetic judgment are then subordinated to the needs of national service in wartime—witness the wartime edition of the *Oxford Book of English Verse* in which the editor said he was omitting all pessimistic poems because he wanted to include nothing but what would "encourage the crew," a declaration of purpose which Mao Tse-tung could approve. If the capitalist powers are entitled to act in this way in time of war, the revolutionary, being permanently on a war footing, is entitled to mobilize writers permanently.

This argument has a factual basis, in that revolutionary experience both resembles and includes war experience, and produces similar demands and a similar psychology. It is also a dangerous argument in that it offers a metaphorical justification for extending, into peace, procedures normal in time of war. It is a form of rhetoric that dates from the first year of the French Revolution, and its dangerous implications were immediately perceived by Edmund Burke. To the extent that capitalist countries do drop in peacetime many of their wartime procedures, this is to their credit, or rather it is an index of the security and sophistication they have, by their energy and rapacity, achieved. The real present weaknesses of the moral position of the intellectual community in the capitalist countries lie elsewhere. I should like to try to outline some of them.

The freedoms that writers and scholars possess in the capitalist world are on a much narrower basis than many Western writers like to suggest. They are in fact an appanage of the rich and moderately rich strata and areas in that world. Most of the population lives in the tributary territories of the so-called underdeveloped world, which is really the poor part of the capitalist world, and there such freedoms usually do not exist. In Latin America, Africa, the Middle East, and Southeast Asia, governments propped up by Western interests are often as repressive in relation to intellectual and other forms of individual liberty as communist governments can be, but without the communist justification in terms of social responsibility and economic and educational achievement. Western governments, which are quite ready to intervene in the internal politics of these countries "in order to prevent the spread of communism," show little disposition to restrain those activities, on the part of anticommunist governments, which most resemble the communist practices to which they like to take public exception. They make clear thereby that their real objection to communism is not to its repressive practices but on the contrary to its positive social content, and to the fact that its extension would make the relation of the principal capitalist centers to the resources of the underdeveloped world less profitable and more onerous than it is when these resources are within the nominal sovereignty of malleable states. In fact these areas are underdeveloped only in relation to the needs of the people who live there. In relation to the demands of the advanced capitalist countries their development is satisfactory in terms of cheap raw materials and high yields on investments.

The Western powers are developing increasingly so-
phisticated means of maintaining these relationships,
through diplomatic pressures, intelligence activity, a
wide range of corruption, intimidation, and in the last
resort such measures as subsidized and guided insurrec-
tion, as in Guatemala, or open military intervention as
in Gabon, the Congo, Santo Domingo, and Vietnam.
These measures are covered by a rhetoric of freedom:
the freedom of the hemisphere, the free world, the
freedom of South Vietnam, the Free Cuba movement.
The alternative instruments of this special kind of freedom are rigged elections and military dictatorships—
sometimes both simultaneously, as in Vietnam. Opposition leaders, if they cannot be bought, will be branded
as communists and be liable to meet the fate of Félix
Moumié, Patrice Lumumba, and countless Indonesians.

The intellectual community to which we belong,
and whose morality we are discussing, is that of the
advanced, capitalist world. In the degree to which it
accepts a moral and social responsibility, that responsibility presumably extends to the whole sphere of activity of the society of which it is part. Professor Frye,
going in a sense further, has said that "the only abiding
loyalty is one to mankind as a whole." The principle is
surely sound, though the expression in practice of
"loyalty to mankind" is extremely difficult, since one's
conception of what is good for mankind is conditioned
by one's own culture, nationality, and class, even when
one speaks in terms of transcending such limitations.
But if we are to move in the direction of a meaningful

loyalty to mankind, the first step must be the realization of moral responsibility in relation to those regions over which our society has power—open economic and partly concealed political power. That is to say, if the intellectual community is going to be moral at all, its morality, whatever form it takes, must concern itself with those great and populous regions which live, to use Graham Greene's words, "in the shadow of your great country." On postulates of morality and responsibility, imaginations should be haunted by these regions and their peoples. On the same postulates, intellects should be preoccupied with their problems, especially their relationships with our own society. In practice, in proportion to the scale of the human problems in question, imaginative interest has been rather rare and independent intellectual interest small. Other kinds of intellectual interest I shall consider separately. So far as imaginative writing in English in the advanced world is concerned, I can think of only two recent works, both novels, about contemporary realities, as distinct from tropical fantasies, in the underdeveloped world. One is Graham Greene's *The Comedians* (about Haiti); the other is David Caute's *Decline of the West* (about an African state resembling in some ways the Congo). Mr. Caute's book is more detailed, and placed nearer to a native perspective, than Mr. Greene's. It was vehemently attacked by some reviewers, and the grounds of attack were revealing of some Western intellectual attitudes toward this area. It was suggested that Mr. Caute had chosen an unfortunate subject, and had become unnecessarily excited about it; that the story was melodramatic and that, although melodramatic things undoubtedly happened in such countries, their happening there does not necessarily make them interesting. The tone of some of these comments conveyed that the critics had little interest in persons whom they considered to be savages, and even less interest in what might be done to these savages on our behalf.

It is not my purpose here to defend Mr. Caute's book. The matter is of interest, in the present context, only as indicative of some geographic and other limitations on the sense of responsibility, and range of imaginative sympathy, of some Western intellectuals. (I hasten to say that I have no program for requiring imaginative writers to write about underdeveloped countries. They write about what interests them, and I suspect that Mary Wollstonecraft's reproach to Burke on the antisocial character of the imagination applies: "I know indeed that there is something disgusting in the distresses of poverty, at which the imagination revolts, and starts back to exercise itself in the more attractive Arcadia of fiction." [2] It is an observation which might well be allowed for in assessing the political opinions and indifferences of certain great imaginative writers—Yeats, Eliot, Claudel.)

As far as intellectual interest in this area is concerned, the situation is different, but in some ways even

[2] *Vindication of the Rights of Men* (1790).

more disquieting. Scholars, in this country especially, have carried out a great number of studies of the economies and social and political structures of underdeveloped countries. Some of these studies are genuine contributions to knowledge, sometimes extremely valuable ones; but some, considerably more numerous in the political field, are not only not contributions to knowledge, but are actually subtractions from it in that they present a false picture of the countries concerned. The specific distortions are the magnification of communist activity and, especially, the minimizing of Western activity. So-called studies of the political life of certain countries, which are known to be dominated by the United States, present an otherwise exhaustively detailed picture of the country, leaving out the United States. Similarly, certain studies of the United Nations blur the reality of the pervasive influence of the United States in the General Assembly and Secretariat. The result is not scholarship but mystification with scholarly apparatus. And even works of genuine scholarship, really enlightening in many ways, are sometimes, indeed often, touched by unscholarly circumlocution when they approach the delicate region of "relations with the United States."

Sometimes these phenomena derive from the natural bent of individual writers: some scholars genuinely find it hard to see the international activities of their own country as an object of study, in the same sense as the international activities of other countries. But the new factor is that such proclivities are now heavily reinforced, and different proclivities discouraged, by the way in which international political studies are today supported and organized. Many of these studies, both respectable and other, are financed either by some branch of the United States government or by some foundation whose politics are the same as those of the United States government, from which it may even acquire its highest personnel. When we find that many of these studies also distort reality, in a sense favorable to U.S. policy and reassuring to U.S. opinion, it is apparent that here the morality of scholarship has been exposed to temptation and in some cases has succumbed with enthusiasm.

Social and political studies have, for obvious reasons, been most affected by the kind of manipulation I have described, but other aspects of our culture are also seriously affected, though less obviously. Studies of contemporary Russian, Chinese, or Arabic literature are politically sensitive. There is a whole set of remarkably similar intellectual reviews in several languages, all of which discuss art, literature, and politics, with the views on art and literature unpredictable and the politics predictably consistent with the foreign policy of the United States; in general, the cultural-political context is such that a noted scholar, seeking support for a program of teaching English as a second language, has judged it expedient to make, as his first claim on behalf of Shakespeare's tongue, the assertion that it is "a bastion against communism."

Since the ultimate object of such activities, on the

part of the United States government, is to prevent revolution, those scholars who lend themselves—if that is the right word—to these activities are accepting, though not proclaiming, the principle of *counterrevolutionary subordination.* The fact that this principle is now quite widely accepted, in practice, in relation to the study of the politics of the most crucial regions, and is more subtly reflected in certain other studies, has, I think, important implications in the framework of our present discussion. Scholarly integrity, and the values it protects, have been *openly* flouted in other countries in revolutionary and postrevolutionary situations. Western scholars have legitimately condemned these goings-on, and if in the course of doing so they have tended to assume a moral altitude higher than any actually attained by our society they are scarcely to be blamed; it is sometimes necessary to condemn and it is hard to condemn without implying a high altitude. But which is more urgent now: to go on condemning what we have already condemned, and can do nothing to change; or to take note of dangers to scholarly integrity arising within our own society, and do what we can—which in this case is something—to repel these dangers?

I am assuming, on good grounds, that revolution in this country is so unlikely as scarcely to require serious consideration, but that the continued promotion by this country of counterrevolution abroad is so likely, so formidable in its resources, so protean in its variety of guises, so deceptive in its reflections in the domestic consciousness, and so dangerous in its long-term implications as to warrant the most sustained and wary attention our minds can give it. This is what we are going to have to live with; it is time we got to know it a little better.

The real danger, here and now, to scholarly integrity as to much else, comes not from *revolutionary subordination*—of which in one form or another we hear much—but from *counterrevolutionary subordination*—of which we hear almost nothing.

It is not just a question of danger to scholarly integrity as a value in itself. It is a question of the impairment of a function which, since it determines our knowledge of our relation to so large a part of our environment, and since the nature of that relation may affect our survival, may without exaggeration be called a vital function. The impairment is serious because, when it is a question of information about distant countries and little-known people, the bad tends not so much to drive out the good as to swamp it. In relation to any given region, there will be published some serious, probing work and some—usually more—work marked by consistently selective myopia. Both will be published under equally respectable imprints and auspices, and will be treated with equal seriousness by reviewers. Anyone struggling to understand the region can only be hopelessly confused by this medley of the true and the misleading. It will not be easy to prevent further obfuscations. Power in our time has more intelligence in its service, and allows that intelligence more discretion as to its methods, than ever before in history. That sounds as if it might be an encouraging thought; myself I find it evocative of one of those sinister utopias—or dystopias, as Professor Frye has said—in this case of a society maimed through the systematic corruption of its intelligence, to the accompaniment of piped music. Obviously we have not come anywhere near that point; we have, however, moved perceptibly in that direction and are likely to move further. The main reason why we are likely to move further is that young scholars are peculiarly sensitive to the kinds of pressure involved. Young scholars in the sensitive fields are likely to believe that if they write with excessive candor about certain realities of political and international life, doors will close to them: certain grants will be out of reach, participation in certain organized research programs denied, influential people alienated, the view propagated that the young man is unbalanced or unsound. These fears may be exaggerated—they often are—but they are not without foundation (I think that is the *mot juste*). Inevitably some young men, many perhaps, will adapt to this situation with such concessions as they believe are necessary. And the scholars who adapt successfully are likely to be highly influential in their fields in the next generation. If we take the title of our symposium seriously, surely increased and specific vigilance, not just the elaboration of general principles, is required from the intellectual community toward specific growing dangers to its integrity. There are indeed some welcome signs of such increased vigilance, especially as regards the relation of universities to government-sponsored research. But modern power is extraordinarily flexible in its methods and resourceful in its reaction to criticisms and reverses, and it would be unwise to assume that even this battle has been won.

On this question of the morality of scholarship, I have discussed only one set of aspects, those that relate to power and politics, revolution and counterrevolution. This choice reflects, obviously, my own present preoccupations, and these in turn are determined by certain experiences in the United Nations and Africa. Not only, however (and not immediately), by those experiences in themselves, but also, immediately, by reading certain academic studies of United Nations and African situations which I knew at first hand, and by finding these studies, in whole or in part, distorted by common and consistent patterns of significant omissions and unwarranted assumptions, all tending to a specific political result. The picture gave me what one might call a shock of nonrecognition. This shock was followed by the reflections which I have just shared with you in the hope that you will bring more of your attention to bear on the present and developing relationship between power in this society and the morality of scholarship.

The Authors

Northrop Frye was born in 1912. He was educated at Victoria College, Toronto, and Oxford University. He was ordained in the United Church of Canada in 1936. He joined the Victoria faculty as Lecturer in English in 1939, became Chairman of the Department of English in 1952 and Principal of the College in 1959. He has been a visiting professor at Harvard, Princeton, Columbia, Indiana, Washington, and British Columbia. In 1967 he resigned the Principalship and was appointed a University Professor in the University of Toronto.

He has been a fellow of the Royal Society of Canada since 1951 and received the Society's Lorne Pierce Medal for distinguished contributions to Canadian literature (1958). He is a former chairman of the English Institute and was a member of the Executive Council of the Modern Languages Association of America. From 1948 to 1952, he was editor of *Canadian Forum*. His writings include *Fearful Symmetry* (1947) and *Anatomy of Criticism* (1957).

Stuart Newton Hampshire was born in 1914 and educated at Repton and Balliol College, Oxford. He came to Princeton as Professor of Philosophy in 1963 from the University of London, where he was Grote Professor of Philosophy of Mind and Logic. He was named chairman of Princeton's Department of Philosophy a year later.

He served as personal assistant to the Minister of State for the Foreign Office in 1945. Most of his teaching career was spent at All Souls College, Oxford, until he joined the London faculty in 1960. He was elected a fellow of the British Academy in that year. He has written *Spinoza* (1951), *Thought and Action* (1959), and *Freedom of the Individual* (1966).

Conor Cruise O'Brien was born in 1917 and educated at Trinity College, Dublin (Ph.D.). He entered Ireland's Department of External Affairs in 1944 and served as counselor in Paris (1955–1956). He was Head of section and a member of the Irish delegation to the United Nations (1956–1960) before being named Assistant Secretary-General of the Department of External Affairs of Ireland in 1960.

O'Brien was the representative of the U.N. Secretary-general in Katanga, Congo, in the crisis following the attempted secession of that province, resigned from the United Nations and the Irish Service (1961) and later served in Africa as Vice-Chancellor of the University of Ghana. He was appointed a Regents Professor at New York University in 1965, when he accepted the Albert Schweitzer Chair in the Humanities.

His books include *Maria Cross* (1952), *Parnell and His Party* (1957), *To Katanga and Back* (1962), and *Writers and Politics* (1965).

Max Black was born in 1909 and educated at Cambridge University, Göttingen and London (Ph.D., D.Lit.). He has been a professor of philosophy at Cornell since 1946, Susan Linn Sage Professor since 1954, and Director of the Society for the Humanities since 1965. He previously taught at the London University Institute of Education and at the University of Illinois, and has been a visiting professor at Kyoto University, Japan; the Hebrew University, Jerusalem; and the Australian National University.

He has been a president of the American Philosophical Association, Eastern Division, and is now a member of the Institut Internationale de Philosophie. He is a fellow of the American Academy of Arts and Sciences.

His latest book is *A Companion to Wittgenstein's Tractatus* (1965).

The Society for the Humanities

The Society for the Humanities was established at Cornell University in 1966 to encourage and support imaginative teaching and research in the humanities. It is intended to be at once a research institute, an experimental college, and a learned society.

Fellows are appointed in three categories: Senior Visiting Fellows, Faculty Fellows, and Junior (postdoctoral) Fellows. The fellowships are held for a year or, occasionally, for shorter terms. The Society also sponsors shorter visits by distinguished humanists. Eventually it is hoped that the activities of the Society will include the establishment of a learned society or academy, concerned with problems of interest to all the humanities.

The Society's aims are philosophical, in concentrating upon the definition and justification of basic principles, and upon the clarification of essential humanistic concepts. Its aims are also practical, in the sense of constantly stressing possible application to urgent human problems. It wishes to encourage serious and sustained argument between conversable teachers and learners, at all levels of maturity. It seeks to make the outcome of such discussion widely available through experimental teaching and by means of publication.

The rubric "humanities" is here deliberately conceived in the broadest possible fashion, to include history and political theory as well as the subjects traditionally counted as humanities: English and foreign literatures, the classics, and philosophy. Nor are the fine arts and the sciences excluded. The tests of relevance are method and attitude of investigation, rather than subject matter.